Carol and Kaya

An Introduction To
Animal Assisted
Therapy and Psychotherapy

CAROL TANNEN, MSW, LCSW

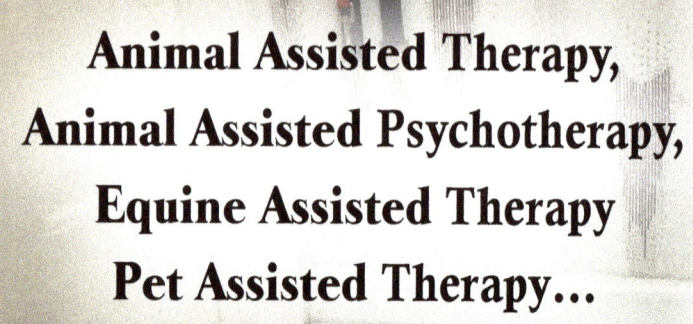

Animal Assisted Therapy,
Animal Assisted Psychotherapy,
Equine Assisted Therapy
Pet Assisted Therapy…

WHAT IS IT ALL ABOUT?

HOW DOES IT WORK?

IS IT FOR ME OR SOMEONE I KNOW?

What is Animal Assisted Therapy?
Copyright © 2019 Carol Tannen, MSW, LCSW

Cover by www.Delaney-Designs.com

This book, Pet Honor Rings and
Animal Assisted Therapy program information available at:
www.AnimalsBringChange.com

Horses, Dogs, and Cats are part of the Therapy Team

Other animals can also be part of the team…

The snake and rat are big hits!

Table of Contents

Prologue 11

Introduction 15

What are the differences between Equine/Pet Therapy, Animal Assisted Therapy and Animal Assisted Psychotherapy? 19

Will I be riding a horse or staying on the ground? 23

Therapy Animals 25

The Therapy Process 31

Addressing Fear of Animals 35

Client Benefits 37

Corporate Benefits 41

Planning a Session… Coming up with Ideas 43

Examples 49

How can I find a Therapist? 57

How can I become a Provider? 59

Personal Stories from Clients… The Impact of Pets 61

From the Pet's Perspective 65

Conclusion 69

The Staff at Animals Bring Change 71

Staff Photos 72

About the Author 77

Prologue

I am a pet lover and the founder of *Animals Bring Change*, a provider of Animal Assisted Therapies. I was introduced to the world of Equine Assisted Psychotherapy in 2010 through a companion at the barn where I board my horse. She had started a program for Equine Assisted Therapy and was working with children with special needs as well as adults with anxieties, eating disorders and addiction issues. She was certified by an organization that is a leader in the field of Equine Assisted Psychotherapy and shared her knowledge and training with me. I joined her in providing therapy sessions and learned how valuable this modality can be. When she eventually moved away, I worked with another certified Equine Therapist and learned even more about the benefits of Equine Assisted Psychotherapy. In order to continue providing this very special therapy, I founded *Animals Bring Change: The ABC's of personal growth through Equine and Pet Assisted Psychotherapy.*

My horse, Kaya, has been my primary animal co-therapist. At times, I have also brought in other horses of various sizes and temperaments based on the activity I have planned for a particular session.

Through the years, I have also worked with other mental health, special education and nursing professionals. Each one has their unique skills and perspectives to contribute and I have found that there is always something new to learn.

One day, after an Equine Therapy Group with an addiction center, the Director asked me if I could offer Canine Therapy at their inpatient facility. I said yes and that was the beginning of my Pet Assisted Psychotherapy Program. I initially brought my dog, Bandit, to their inpatient facility. With Bandit as my co-therapist, we offered Pet Assisted Group Therapy that we structured similarly to the Equine program.

When I got another dog, Maggie, she joined our team. She added another dimension to the sessions by having two dogs with very different personalities

A short time later, I rescued 2 kittens, brothers Rahj and Duke, who came to many sessions with me.

Sometimes I brought my older cat, Chloe, until she sadly passed away of old age.

My daughter, Courtney, added a small ball python snake to our family of pets, so Arcturus the Snake has also been a participant in many sessions. He has enabled several clients to overcome their fear of snakes and realize they can overcome other personal fears as well.

Our latest addition is a pet rat. One of the drawbacks for me about having a snake around is that he has to eat. Unfortunately, this means having a small mouse or small rat for dinner every week or so. However, one of these potential dinners was very smart and stood quietly against the side wall of the snake's glass enclosure, not moving. My daughter noticed this and felt like the rat was "looking into my soul and telling me today is not her day to die." So she took her out of the snake's enclosure and Voila! We now have an adorable pet rat named Ratilda. Here she is on her first day of freedom.

Through *Animals Bring Change*, I have the opportunity to combine my therapeutic skills as a Social Worker with my love and understanding of horses and other animals.

I recently attended a presentation by my college alma mater, Syracuse University, and the speaker was updating us on the school. During her speech, she smiled and commented "and can you believe it, they're even providing pet therapy!" I went over to her afterwards and I said "Yes, I can believe that. I actually provide pet assisted therapy myself." We talked about how effective and beneficial it will be for the students and staff alike.

My impression is that a lot of people have heard of the concept of Animal Assisted Therapy, but don't really understand what it is or what to expect, and that's what prompted me to write this book.

With the variety of clients and pets, as well as differing activities, every therapy session is unique. Every participant walks away with their own personal experience and result. Equine and Pet Assisted Therapy can have an amazing positive and lasting effect on everybody.

I hope you enjoy reading about Equine and Pet Assisted Therapy as much as I enjoy providing it.

Introduction

Your dog wags its tail when you walk in the door…..you smile and feel happy.

You walk into the pasture and your horse trots over to greet you…..you feel appreciated.

Your kitten curls up on your lap…..you feel loved.

Such simple acts, but such powerful moments!

Every day, people are affected by the animals that surround them. What if you could channel that power into healing your soul, opening your mind, and increasing awareness of your own behavior towards others? This is what Animal Assisted Therapy does. Horses, dogs, cats and other animals ASSIST us in increasing our awareness of our own behavior. They look past our words and tune into our body language, which shows our true selves.

Think about a personal experience you have had with an animal. Was it positive or negative? How did it make you feel? What effect did it have on you at that time and how has it affected you in the long term. Has it changed you in any way?

This experience will give you more insight into the world of animal assisted therapies. We work through both the positive and negative experiences and look at them from a new perspective.

Families, individuals and groups can all benefit from interacting with animals and with each other, learning to recognize the effects of behaviors in the bigger picture.

As an example, the first time meeting a horse you walk over and put out your hand for the horse to smell – like you would a dog. But the horse thinks you are giving him a treat. When he sees no treat, he backs away from you. A simple scenario, right? However, you immediately think the horse backed away because he doesn't like you, so, feeling hurt, you move on to the next horse. If you look at this from another perspective though, the horse simply had expectations that weren't met so he was disappointed. It wasn't personal about YOU. Think of what might have occurred if you had stayed and moved towards the horse and petted him. Compare this to meeting a person for the first time and you come to the realization that sometimes you make assumptions and move on without giving the other person a second chance or even time to explain themselves. No wonder your life can get lonely sometimes!

Now, imagine you're training your new puppy to jump over a bar. You set it 2 feet off the ground and instead of jumping, he goes under it. You feel like a failure. Someone suggests lowering the bar, so you set it 6 inches off the ground and the puppy jumps over it! You realize you may need to take smaller steps to achieve the goals in your own life.

Cats... No way! I don't like cats! But you're not even sure why. So you finally convince yourself to take a chance and let a little kitten sit on your lap. He snuggles and starts to purr. You pet him and find yourself feeling calm and nurturing. Hmmmmm.... Maybe cats aren't so bad after all. Maybe you need to give yourself a chance to try new things more often.

These are just some of the ways that **Animals Bring Change** to people's lives. The use of horses, dogs, kittens, etc. has been gaining traction in the world of therapy... physical therapy, psychotherapy, child therapy, therapy with Veterans with PTSD, therapy with seniors, and more. There are so many wonderful opportunities for the interactions between animals and humans to provide personal growth, improve outlooks on life, and offer comfort!

Animal therapies are experiential, nonjudgmental opportunities to explore personal behaviors and attitudes. They help people learn life skills, understand what makes them tick, and recognize how they come across to others. Animals tune in to our emotions without us having to say anything, giving us immediate feedback on deeper feelings we may not even be aware of. This interaction helps people see how their behaviors affect other people, and see how their interpretation of someone else's behavior can affect their own mood and feelings of self-worth.

What are the differences between Equine/Pet Therapy, Animal Assisted Therapy & Animal Assisted Psychotherapy?

As a general term, EQUINE/PET THERAPY means many things. It can mean a horse or pet needs therapy; it can mean bringing a horse or pet to a nursing home or school; it can mean involving a horse or pet in a psychotherapy session. When I mention "Equine/Pet Therapy" to people, I get asked questions about what it is. To clear up the confusion, I do not use the term to mean that my horse or pet needs therapy. I use it to mean that my horse and pets assist me in providing therapy to others. The terminology most used today tends to be Animal Assisted Therapy and Animal Assisted Psychotherapy.

ANIMAL ASSISTED THERAPY utilizes the unique characteristics of animals to help people with autism, special needs, emotional issues, and physical challenges. It has also been found to be comforting to the elderly in nursing homes and to children experiencing loss, stress or other issues in schools. Petting the animals, reading to them, grooming and touching them, and physically mounting and riding a horse all fit in this category. Interactions with animals can reduce stress levels and provide comfort. Horseback riding can help improve balance and muscle tone in physically challenged individuals.

ANIMAL ASSISTED PSYCHOTHERAPY takes this in a slightly different direction to deal more specifically with psychological issues. Involving animals in psychotherapy sessions enables clients to get immediate feedback directly from the animal. How the animal responds to a person's actions, like backing away if a person approaches too quickly or aggressively, can point out how that person's behavior may be affecting other people he or she interacts with. There are also times when people are encouraged to talk to the animals and share stories they find difficult to open up about with a therapist or family member. For the purpose of understanding what's behind the animal assisted psychotherapy concept, imagine that the horse is a metaphor for your own personal experience. Your name, gender, history, etc. isn't important for now. For now, you are here in the moment, interacting with the horse and realizing he is giving you feedback and insight into your behavior and picking up on your feelings. For example, your therapist gives you directions to engage in a particular activity with the horse, such as "Use the props provided to build an obstacle course. Label the obstacles with your goals, then take the horse through the obstacle course."

There are no further instructions…it is up to you to figure out what to do. This is not a contest or a competition so what you do is based on your own personal interpretation. You find that the horse stops at one of your obstacles and you realize that's the one where you are most stuck in life, the one that's keeping you from achieving your goals. How did the horse know? Horses are very intuitive and can read us better than we know ourselves. The therapist will observe and then may process your activity with you when you have completed it. This discussion allows you to explore what has gone on and understand it more fully.

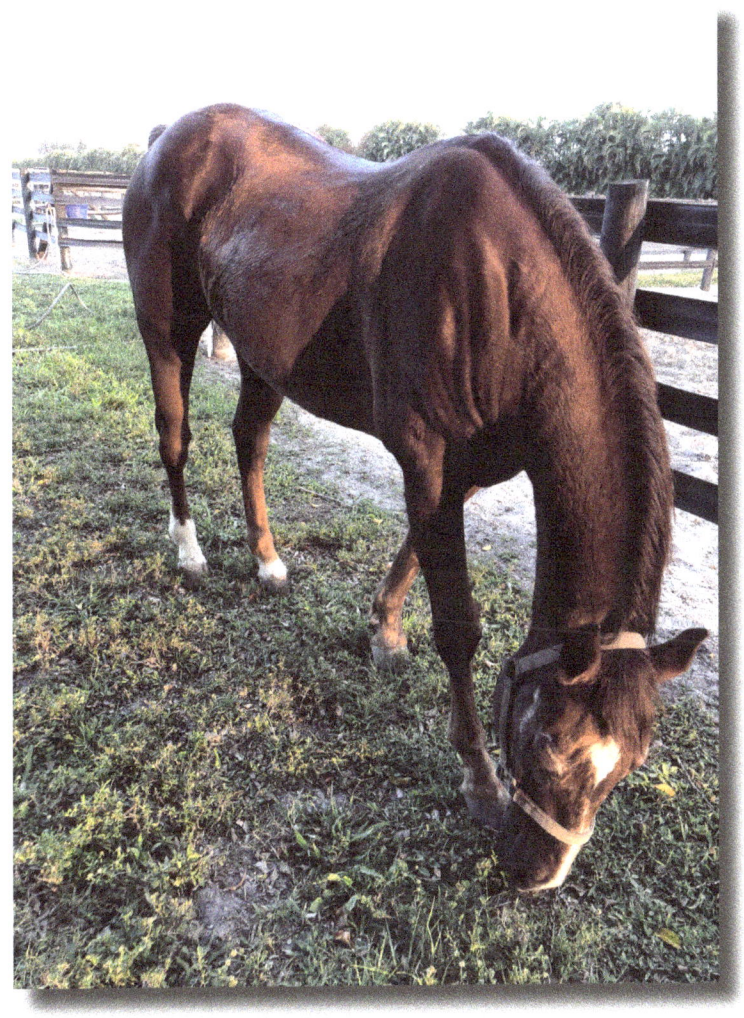

Will I be Riding a Horse or Staying on the Ground?

A very common question is "Will I be riding a horse in an Equine Assisted Program?" This requires both a YES and NO answer.

YES - Riding the horse can be very beneficial for people with physical disabilities. The movement of the horse mimics the motion of the body and strengthens the muscles. This is called Hippotherapy and it improves coordination, balance and strength. Riding is also helpful with autism and speech issues because children can work on saying simple words like "go" and "stop." I will stand next to the horse and wait patiently until children say something to indicate they want the horse to move before I will start walking. This encourages them to speak. Riding also enables riders to feel tall and empowered, seeing the world around them from a new perspective.

NO - Staying on the ground and being involved in activities with the horses is the typical method for Equine Assisted Psychotherapy. Being able to touch and pet the horse, groom the horse, walk the horse around, take the horse over an obstacle course, paint the horse, etc. are all activities that help with bonding and understanding the horse and oneself. Being on the ground, instead of riding, also allows a couple, family or individual to interact in a structured setting without worrying about their riding ability.

Therapy Animals

Who are they? What are their qualifications? What makes a good therapy animal?

Simply put, a good therapy animal has a loving heart, likes to be around people, tunes into feelings and enjoys the job.

The characteristics of a good therapy animal include being kind, safe, fun, and having an obvious personality. For example, I have two dogs that have very different personalities. One walks into a room, visits everybody and loves to play ball or tug of war. The other dog is quiet and shy, waits for people to come over to pet her and isn't interested in toys. Whether the animal is friendly or shy, both work for different people who can relate to one or the other. Even an aging pet can provide an opportunity to connect with people dealing with similar issues such as illness and physically slowing down.

Dogs, cats, horses, and many other animals can be involved in Animal Assisted Therapy. I have a snake that attends group therapy sessions in an addiction center and he helps people overcome their fears and deal with their anxiety. My pet rat likes sitting on a shoulder and hanging out. One important factor is to be careful which animals are brought to a therapy session together. My dogs get along well with the cats, horses, snake and rat. However I would never bring the snake and rat together. Obviously the snake would try to eat the rat, but there's also another reason. If the snake smells the rat on someone who was just holding her, he might mistake that person for the rat and think that person's hand is his food. Safety of both the animals and the people is always the number one priority!

In this photo, you can see that Maggie and Kaya are fine together, as they are enjoying grazing side by side.

One of the most confusing issues for people is: What are the differences between THERAPY animals, EMOTIONAL SUPPORT animals and SERVICE animals? Typically, these animals are dogs, but horses and other animals are now also a part of this concept. There are major differences between the three categories.

THERAPY animals are not required to have any specific skill training but are expected to behave well around people and other animals without biting or being aggressive. They are not legally entitled to the special treatment that EMOTIONAL SUPPORT animals and SERVICE animals are. They are THERAPY animals because they participate in a variety of programs where it is therapeutic for people to be around them. For example, having a dog present in the office during an individual or family therapy session can be soothing and productive. It allows clients to find comfort and strength from petting the dog, while addressing their own problems.

Animal Assisted Psychotherapy groups involve sessions with THERAPY animals that enable people to interact with them, engage in a structured activity with them, and experience their reactions…which can help them see their behavior and consequences in their personal relationships with people. In psychotherapy settings, the animals help with problem resolution and personal growth.

THERAPY animals are often brought in to nursing homes to walk around and visit with people. In these settings, they provide support and comfort by giving people a chance to pet them, and spend time with them. Many of the residents miss their own pets and relish this opportunity to give and get pet love again. THERAPY animals also go to schools to sit with children so the children can practice reading to them. In addition, THERAPY animals are often brought to a location to relieve stress and anxiety after a crisis situation.

In some situations, the Mental Health Therapist works with an Animal Specialist, someone familiar with the animals who can look out for the welfare of both the animals and the people. My daughter, Courtney, works with me as the Animal Specialist for various therapy programs. When her Grandfather lived in a nursing home near one of the facilities where we ran a weekly group, we would bring the dogs and small ball python snake over to visit him. Her Grandfather liked to call the snake "Jake the Snake." In this photo, they are enjoying a walk through his nursing home with the dogs, Maggie and Bandit.

The nursing home residents in the hallways would constantly stop us so they could pet the dogs and tell us stories about the pets they used to have. Sometimes there were even some brave souls who wanted to hold the snake.

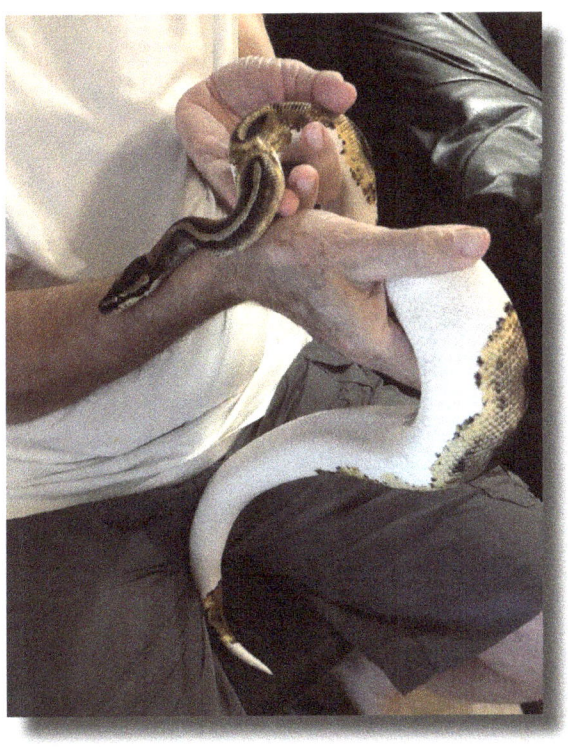

EMOTIONAL SUPPORT animals help people with feelings of anxiety, depression and loneliness by being a companion. They don't need any particular training so many animals qualify in this category. Dogs, cats, birds, hamsters, etc. can be EMOTIONAL SUPPORT animals. With a letter from a medical doctor or mental health professional documenting that a person has an emotional need, EMOTIONAL SUPPORT animals are now allowed to live in buildings where pets are typically prohibited. EMOTIONAL SUPPORT dogs and other animals have been allowed in the cabins on airplanes, but there are restrictions as to what animals are allowed, and which flights they can go on. The airlines are currently working to clarify their rules and are becoming stricter about letting animals onboard.

SERVICE animals require intense long term training to be taught to perform a variety of specific tasks. When SERVICE animals are working, they should not be petted or distracted because this could cause them to miss cues that could risk the life of their human companion. They may warn someone that a seizure is coming, they may pick up things for someone in a wheelchair, they may help a blind person walk around and cross the street. SERVICE animals are the only ones who are allowed to be with their companion 24/7 in all settings because often the person's life depends on them. You may notice them in stores and restaurants. Airlines have allowed SERVICE animals to accompany their handlers in the airplane cabin but are becoming increasingly strict about the rules and the length of the flight they can be on.

The Therapy Process

Most people are familiar with traditional therapy where you meet with a therapist in an office and talk about what is going on that might be troubling you. However, many people are not familiar with Animal Assisted Psychotherapies and wonder what they are all about and how they work.

Animal Assisted Psychotherapy is similar to traditional talk therapy in the sense that the licensed mental health therapist helps individuals deal with various personal and emotional issues. The therapist helps people understand their behavior and their relationships which enables them to gain insight and experience personal growth. The difference in Animal Assisted Therapies is that the therapist incorporates activities with the animals into the therapy sessions. This interaction allows the clients to immediately experience the animal's reactions and feelings, which can mirror or be metaphors for their own behavior. Therapy sessions can take place with an individual, a couple, a family or a group.

Most people immediately think of horses and dogs as Therapy animals, but I have brought cats, a snake and a pet rat into my sessions with wonderful results. While the horses are large and beautiful, they can also sometimes be intimidating, which helps with gaining confidence. The dogs and cats can be playful and charming, bringing out the warm fuzzy feelings. The snake and rat bring out the curiosity and the satisfaction of overcoming fear. The snake likes curling up on a lap or crawling into a warm sweatshirt. The rat enjoys running from chair to chair visiting. She also likes to be cuddly…often sitting on a shoulder and giving little rat kisses on an ear or a cheek.

Here's our rat, Ratilda, enjoying a pat on the back during one of our group therapy sessions.

Animal Assisted Psychotherapy with dogs, cats and small animals, is typically offered by a licensed Mental Health Therapist who may or may not have an Animal Specialist assisting. Since the animals are small and generally easier to handle, the Mental Health Therapist may choose to work alone. In large groups or hippotherapy sessions with horses, where safety is an issue, it is helpful to have an Animal Specialist there. I have personally worked both with and without an Animal Specialist present, depending on the clients and the activities I am doing. Pet Assisted sessions can take place either at a farm or in an office setting.

Equine Assisted Psychotherapy is typically offered by a team consisting of a licensed Mental Health Therapist and an Animal Specialist. The Mental Health Therapist can focus on the psychotherapy aspect of the session while the Animal Specialist is familiar with the horses and can anticipate the horse's behavior and keep everyone safe. This is especially helpful in group sessions because of the size of the horses and the number of people interacting around them. Equine Assisted Therapy sessions take place on a ranch or farm setting. They offer the client an opportunity to interact with the horses and get immediate feedback that helps with personal understanding and growth.

Equine and Pet Assisted Psychotherapy sessions generally follow a structured pattern. The therapist and clients spend some time talking about what issues the clients are experiencing that need to be addressed. Then they discuss what to expect from this experience and, after reviewing safety rules, they are introduced to the horse or pet. Next, the clients are given directions for an interactive experience with the horse or pet. Usually, the therapist will avoid giving too many details or specifics in the directions so that the clients can interpret the directions their own way. It is also important to stress that there are no right or wrong answers. This makes the experience more personal for each participant. During the exercise, the therapist guides the session as needed. After the exercise, the clients and therapist may decide this is a good place to end the session or they may choose to talk more and process what transpired during the interaction. This discussion could include how the clients felt, how they reacted to the animal, and how the animal reacted to them. Through guidance from the therapist, the clients can begin to see and understand the results of their own actions. Each session may be a little different and the structure may vary depending on the situation, the goals and the personal style of the therapist.

Animal Assisted Therapy in schools and nursing homes is typically provided by volunteers who go wherever their pet's love is needed. For example, dogs have been brought to schools when there is a crisis or tragedy and people need emotional support and a calming influence. Dogs go to schools to sit with children who are learning to read so the children can practice reading to them without being embarrassed in front of other children. Some police departments even use pets to gather information about an incident... children may tell a dog what happened when they wouldn't be able to tell an adult directly. They have also been used to comfort and support children who have to testify in court. They offer an opportunity for people to pet the animals, give them love and attention, feel love from them and talk to them. The animals provide comfort and security in all of these settings.

Addressing Fear of Animals

Afraid of animals? Had a bad experience in the past? First of all, CONGRATULATIONS for coming to a session and facing your fear! If you can face it here, you can develop strategies for facing other fears in your daily life. By the end of the session you may have petted the horse, held the cat, walked the dog, touched the snake… What a feeling of accomplishment!

One client said he was afraid of big dogs because he was pushed by one when he was little. He couldn't remember the kind of dog it was, so we discussed how his being so small then could have made even a little dog look big.

He laughed at the thought it might have just been a Chihuahua and started to look at his fear from a more rational adult perspective.

Many people are afraid of snakes and I was hesitant to include my daughter's new baby ball python snake, Arcturus, in our therapy sessions at an addiction center. However, she convinced me to try it and to my surprise, he was very well received.

It turned out that there were many people in the group who have had snakes and were excited to hold one again. Of course, there were also some who wanted to sit on the other side of the room or bail altogether. The scared and reluctant ones were also very curious and, once they calmed down, wanted to touch or pet or even hold the snake. Their pride at this accomplishment and their ability to overcome their fear had a lasting positive effect on them.

As a therapist, there can be fears as well. Picture this! It's your first day visiting at a nursing home....You groomed your dog, you know Bentley is sweet and friendly, you look forward to the attention and loving he'll bring to the residents. So you proudly walk through the front door and suddenly... Your dog poops on the floor! Evidently he's as nervous as you are for his first day on the job! Totally embarrassed, do you laugh, cry, run back home??? Nah, might as well just clean it up and keep going! The rest of the day turns out to be a success and they invite you back again next week. Only next time, you make sure to take the dog for a long walk first!

Client Benefits

The benefit of Animal Assisted Therapy that differentiates it from traditional talk therapy is that the animals mirror and/or react to a person's behavior in an immediate way. This reaction provides the client with immediate feedback and offers a visual picture of the pet's reaction they can keep with them long after the therapy session is over. For example, a client quickly reaches down and tries to pick up a dog before making any other efforts to greet it. The dog's reaction is to back away, startled. The client sees that this behavior came across as too sudden and aggressive for the dog to respond positively to it. In processing this experience, the client realizes he's often too aggressive in his interpersonal relationships and this tends to push people away.

Sometimes talk therapy can get to a point where a client or family feels like they're at a plateau. A few sessions of Equine or Pet Assisted Therapy may get things moving again. For example, a family is having difficulty resolving some issues so they decide to attend an Equine Assisted Psychotherapy session. They are given a saddle and bridle and asked to put them on the horse. Having no previous experience doing this, they make an effort and you can rapidly see the family dynamics become evident. Maybe one person tries to lead or boss the family around, maybe one person steps back and watches, maybe one starts arguing about another way it can be done. The therapist then shares observations, such as "I noticed you were taking the lead. How did your family respond?" Through observation and nonjudgmental guidance, the therapist opens the door for the family to see their effects on each other and experience emotions in the here and now.

A detailed history of the client is not as important or necessary in this form of therapy because this form of therapy works with the client wherever they are at this moment, at this point in time. The focus is on their feelings during the current experience. Their personal growth comes from their own assessment of their reactions and behavior.

How does change happen? Where does insight come from? Can change be permanent? How does it feel to have an "AHA!" moment? And what does all this have to do with animals? Animals tend to respond to our behavior, to sense our innermost thoughts and feelings – especially the ones we can't always necessarily express in words. They pick up on our feelings, our attitudes, and our fears. They read nonverbal language very well. Interactions with animals can shed light on our own behaviors. How an animal reacts is often how others are reacting to us, but we don't always want to accept it from people the way we can examine ourselves with an animal. If your girlfriend walks away from you, you may feel hurt and angry. If the horse walks away from you, you may say "it doesn't like me" - the hurt shows but the anger isn't there so it's easier to deal with the feelings and the experience more honestly. The conversation with the girlfriend is going to be based more in anger, while the animal interaction is an awareness of feelings. What did you do to make the girlfriend walk away? What did you do to make the horse walk away? Chances are it's from the same basic issue - your style of approaching and interacting with others. Did you burst onto the scene wanting attention? Did you raise your voice and change your tone? Did you walk quickly and get too close too fast? Did you lift your hands in a threatening manner? Examining the events leading up to them walking away from you can help you understand how you come across to others and how your behavior is being interpreted by others.

The human/animal interactions can also be mutually supportive and heartwarming. My dog Maggie was rescued from a shelter where she was given up because she was "shy". When she first started coming in to a group room, she was hesitant and cautious, often hiding under a chair. Over time, she became more comfortable and interactive with everybody.  Now she bounces into a room and makes the rounds greeting everyone. She likes being brushed and petted and seems to tune into the people needing a calming effect. Here's a moment where the human and dog both realize they need a big hug.

Animal Assisted Psychotherapy can be short term or go on for a while. It depends on the goals the client has set and how long it takes to achieve them. Knowing when you have actually accomplished what you set out to do is also an important part of the therapy.

Corporate Benefits

Corporations have many facets, departments and levels of management. Providing a cohesive, comfortable work environment helps everyone feel appreciated and motivated to do their best. Sometimes a cog gets stuck in the wheel and things don't go as smoothly as desired. Sometimes the group works well but there are inherent stresses in the job that could benefit from a stress reliever.

This is where bringing in a pet for a visit could be very beneficial. An opportunity for staff to play with a cat or dog for a while may be enough of a diversion to enable employees to renew their energy and get back to work.

Running a more structured group psychotherapy session in the office setting, involving the pets as co-therapists, is also a good way to deal with problems and get the staff back on track. As an example, each person in the group is asked to train the dog to do a trick. After each person has a turn, you can discuss issues such as: How do you train someone? How do you help each other learn new tasks? Do you exhibit patience, provide clear instructions and have realistic expectations? Another example is observing the dogs for a while and then discussing their behavior. Is one dog in charge? How do you know? Describe your own corporate structure and where you fit in. A third example is asking the group to develop a treatment plan together, such as helping the dogs get out more for exercise and socializing. This can lead to a group bonding experience.

Taking the staff out of the work environment and making a field trip to the barn can also be helpful in many ways. Is teamwork a problem at work? Is someone "bossy"? Is someone "lazy"? Asking the team to observe the interactions of a herd of horses and then write down how they would label each one, opens the door to a discussion about the role each person plays on the team. It helps them see how they can be more cohesive in the future.

The possibilities for improving the work place environment are endless. Sessions involving a structured animal based activity, a chance to pet an animal, a feel good diversion from the work tasks, can have a very positive effect on the business atmosphere.

Planning a Session...
Coming up with Ideas

You may be wondering: What constitutes a therapy session? How many people attend? How long does it last? If it's a session with horses, what happens if it's hot or cold or raining outside? How do the activities differ if the session involves one person or 20 people? Flexibility is crucial! Backup plans are a necessity! For the therapist, having an arsenal of activities ready is really important!

A therapy session can involve one or more people. The time frame can be 30 minutes or one hour or more depending on a variety of factors such as the number of people attending, the activity planned, and the personal style of the therapist. It can also vary depending on whether it's with horses or with small animals, on a farm or in an office setting. And things can change on the spur of the moment.... If the plan was to build an obstacle course for horses in the ring but it starts to rain, you can spend time in the horse stalls instead, experiencing the horses' "room" on a rainy day. You can discuss issues like: Is it comforting and safe or do you feel trapped? How do you handle your boredom on rainy days?

Ideas for a therapy session can come from anywhere and everywhere. Be aware, be creative, be open to ideas. The therapist needs to always be prepared with an activity, but the client can also introduce an idea or question that can end up being what the session is all about. Life experiences, such as sitting in on an AA meeting can provide insight for a session at a drug and alcohol rehabilitation facility. A post you come across on Facebook can be shared and discussed to address any number of social, family and personal issues. A cartoon can bring in a sense of humor to the session.

Bringing an outside experience to the therapy group can make it very real and personal for everybody. For example, if it's a pet's birthday, you can make the session a birthday party. In this photo, Maggie got dressed up for her birthday party. She is wearing a birthday hat decorated by a participant in an addiction rehabilitation center. While they made birthday hats and ate cookies, the group reflected on their own past birthday experiences…good and bad. Many couldn't remember the last time they celebrated their birthdays sober. This party allowed them to have fun and enjoy themselves while sober and helped them look forward to being sober for their own birthdays in the future.

If the group expected to be with the little pony today and the therapist brought out her biggest horse instead, talk about dealing with disappointment. It's a perfect opportunity to learn ways to cope when things don't go the way you hoped they would.

In a sad and unexpected situation where an animal dies, having a grief session can be very helpful and powerful. I ended up doing this at the barn when a horse passed away. The group was used to seeing the horse every week and they knew it was sick. When they arrived one day and noticed that the horse was gone, they were all quite upset. We decided to talk about it and share stories about what they would like to say to people while they're still alive. Several went home and acted on this, making calls they had been afraid to make before.

After watching the Wizard of Oz on TV one night, it became the theme for my next group. Each participant picked the character they wanted to be. Then they acted out their roles as they walked around the ring, which we designated as the yellow brick road to Oz. One participant said "I want to be the tin man because I'm feeling cold and heartless inside." How metaphorical and cathartic for him!

We often let Ratilda, the rat, run loose around the house, and she likes to play with the dogs. We thought it would be a good idea to train her to walk on a leash so she could go outside with them. However, it wasn't as easy as we thought it would be. So we asked the participants in one of our groups to help. They put on the harness and leash and had fun trying to get her to walk with them.

It was a learning opportunity for the group because it took several tries and then a group effort to accomplish the goal. They each took turns trying ideas they thought might work and then the group worked together to put a plan in to action.

Here's a picture of the results.

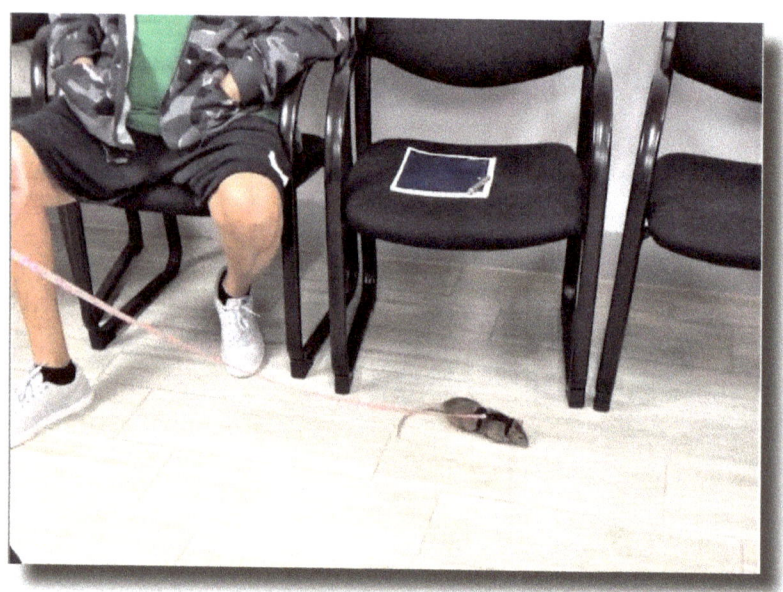

Mixing animals can also be helpful in therapy sessions. Bringing the dogs to the farm to interact with the horses creates a different environment to deal with. Occasionally I have decided to bring one or more of the dogs with me to an equine assisted psychotherapy session to enhance the client's growth. One dog may offer a calming effect while bringing the second dog adds an extra dimension of responsibility and distraction that some clients need to learn to deal with.

It's very important to be open to change in every session. There have been many times when a planned activity never happened because a participant took the session in another direction. For example, walking out to the horse paddock, a group member noticed someone lunging a horse in another ring. Lunging is moving a long whip in the air to keep the horse going in a circle to get exercise. Immediately they thought it was abusive, so we all watched the horse being lunged for a while. The horse was not being harmed but this led to a discussion about when a whip or a bat or anything can be harmful versus useful as a learning tool. In this instance, I went and got all types of horse whips and had the group gently touch the horses with them to pet them. Then they used them to direct the horses to walk in a circle without touching the horses. The abusive whip instead became a useful tool. One client reflected on how he had been hit with a stick as a young boy. It took a lot of encouragement to get him to pick up the whip and gently pet the horse with it. My planned activity never happened but the group got more out of the session because this new activity was more meaningful at that moment in time.

Examples

In a residential rehabilitation center for drug and alcohol addiction, the group anxiously awaits the weekly arrival of the pet therapist. Up until now, the group has enjoyed interacting with the same 2 dogs each week. On this particular day, the therapist enters with 2 tiny kittens instead. The group learns that the kittens were just rescued an hour earlier from another addict who wasn't taking care of them. The discussion centers around their personal experiences of losing their pets because of their own addiction. Seeing the helpless kittens in such a scruffy condition and experiencing how loving and cuddly they are with everyone in spite of this treatment, is an eye opener. It makes the group more aware of how their addiction affects their own innocent and helpless pets. Many leave the session more motivated to succeed and return home to treat their own pets, kids and families better.

In a relationship, have you ever found yourself in a situation where you have to give up control and totally trust another person? How scary was it? To find out, put on a blindfold and lead a horse through an obstacle course, while someone else walks with you and verbally guides you through the course. Some people are better at giving directions than others, so this can become a fun but challenging experience. Some people can keep their eyes closed, others can't help but peek. Issues of trust are then discussed and processed in an equine assisted psychotherapy session.

Have you ever wondered what someone is feeling and you can't quite put your finger on it? A game of charades can be very enlightening. Leading the horse around a ring while acting out a feeling gives your group an opportunity to tune in to you and how you communicate. Did they guess how you're feeling? If not, what did they think you were feeling and how can you express yourself better in the future? During one session, a client was feeling sick so he walked slowly around the ring with his head down, occasionally coughing. When he was done, he stopped in front of the group and the horse coughed! Everyone was surprised at just how tuned in the horse had become to him!

A little 3 year old boy with special needs arrives at the barn having a bad day, throwing a tantrum and running off by himself. First, we work with the family to get this behavior under control. Then, we lift him up on the horse. The moment he gets up on the horse, a big smile comes across his face and he starts to sing and look around at everything.

He loves being a cowboy!

Social interactions are tough for many people, especially those with autism and other special needs. Being around the horse or pet enables a person to interact and feel the comfort of tactile stimulation. Petting and grooming the animal encourages smiles and expressions of happiness. Sometimes, this is the first time a word or emotion is clearly spoken and expressed. What a milestone! Then imagine placing that child with autism, cerebral palsy or low self-esteem up on top of the horse and they feel like they're on top of the world! If they want the horse to move, it's their job to tell the horse to go. For someone who rarely speaks, saying "GO" is a really big deal! Now the therapist starts walking the horse and the rider gets a new view of the world. Want the horse to stop? You better tell him "STOP"! Here comes another spoken word from an otherwise quiet child. The feeling of empowerment is sensational!

A new participant began a session by saying she had heard that lifting a horse's foot, to clean its hooves, meant it trusted you. She acknowledged having trust issues herself and admitted being a little afraid of lifting a horse's leg. So we made that the activity for the session. She was hesitant to approach the horse and it took a while before she could reach down and lift his leg, but she finally did it! She was able to overcome her fear and get the horse to trust her. Her smile and her pride in her accomplishment were heartwarming. Another client who tried the same activity, but couldn't get the horse to lift his leg, said she felt like a failure. I explained to her that it's not about passing or failing, it's about what you learn about yourself.

Do you have trust issues? Do you give up easily? What can you do to change things? It's important to look at the positives in each scenario.

For people struggling with eating disorders, self-perception is very important. One activity I have done is to ask each participant to observe several horses and then write down a guess of each one's weight and girth (inches around the barrel/belly of the body). Then we used a tape measure and compared it to their guesses. When they saw the actual measurements, they were surprised. There was a big difference between their perception and the reality. This opened the door to a great discussion about how people see themselves versus how others see them.

Another activity involved dressing up the horse to go to the place of your choice, to your happy place. We had various props available to use. It was an opportunity to be creative and to think about what makes you feel good about yourself. Here's one result....

This person chose the beach. Kaya's ready!

Have you ever considered how difficult it can be for some people to make new friends? Shy people may find it hard to walk up to someone and say hello. Addicts overcoming their addiction may need to give up their old friends and find new sober friends. A person who recently moved to a new town may not know where to even start to meet new people. Where can you go to meet people? What do you say to someone the first time you meet? One of the group activities that addresses this involves having two people stand up at opposite ends of the room and each takes a dog on a leash. They are instructed to pretend they are going to the dog park, which is in the middle of the room, and then spend 2 minutes interacting with each other. It's interesting to observe the various types of conversations. People who are anxious about meeting others and about performing in front of a group, often surprise themselves with their comfort level and ability to manage to converse for a short time. Many times, the focus of the conversation is on each person introducing their dog and asking questions about the other dog, but they see it's a start. Sometimes they get comfortable enough talking with the other person that they decide to make plans to get together again. This role playing helps build their self-confidence and improve their social and communication skills. Since this takes place in a group setting, it is also a helpful way to overcome the fear of public speaking.

Do you ever think about New Years as a time to get rid of the old and start fresh? Imagine writing down everything you want to get rid of and making it go away! That would be so nice and easy wouldn't it? Well, after writing the "get rid of" list, toss it to Bandit, my dog who loves to rip up paper. As he shreds it into little pieces, you feel a sense of relief that it's gone now and, looking at the floor, you realize you can't possibly put all the little pieces back together.

It's time to finally move on!

My daughter, Courtney, works with me in large group sessions as the Animal Specialist, and she brings another viewpoint and perspective to our sessions. The next picture is her with Bandit, relaxing after a group game of "Being Pawsitive". The paper cups on the floor are filled with pennies. Each person started with a cupful of pennies but every time they said something negative, they had to give up a penny and put it in the center cup. This experience was an eye opener when they realized how many negative comments they were making without realizing it. It also made them become very aware of how negative comments can be hurtful and have consequences.

In an Equine Therapy Group, each person had to walk the horse a few feet, then stop to tell a story about their childhood, then walk and stop to tell about their current life, then walk and stop to tell about their future wishes. They all walked the same horse with no trouble. Then one woman tried and the horse kept walking her to the grass and eating… totally ignoring her. As she told her stories, she complained that no one ever listens or pays attention to her. The horse had picked up on this and was treating her the same way. This became an opportunity for her to gain control of the situation, be stronger and get the horse to walk with her. She was successful and learned about standing up for herself.

Some other experiences include: writing down how you think your pet would describe you; celebrating a pet's birthday and talking about how you spend your own birthdays; seeing the dogs come into the room dressed in various outfits and talking about first impressions; teaching the dog to do a new trick and understanding the process of setting and achieving goals in your own life; writing down the things you learn from a pet and seeing how pets affect your life, such as your sense of responsibility. The list is endless. As simple as these ideas sound, they open the door to gaining insight and can have a huge and lasting impact on personal growth and understanding. These interactions with the animals act as a metaphor for what is actually going on in a person's life.

How Can I Find a Therapist?

Equine and Pet Assisted Therapies are fairly new and novel concepts. Therefore, depending on where you live, Animal Assisted Therapy may or may not be available nearby. Social Workers, Psychologists and Mental Health professionals are the ones who typically provide this form of therapy. There are various organizations that offer training for therapists and may be able to direct you to a local provider. There are also animal assisted therapy programs that focus on children, on dealing with grief, and on veteran specific issues. Looking on the internet may provide some direction by informing you of the programs available in your locale.

An equine or pet therapy provider can be either your primary mental health therapist or can be in a support role with another therapist or program. If you already have a primary therapist, they may be able to refer you to an equine therapist to enhance your growth. Both therapists can work together to help you resolve various issues.

Throughout the years, I have received referrals from other therapists when they feel a client can benefit from hands on experiential type sessions. I have also provided animal assisted therapy sessions to facilities for addictions and for eating disorders as an addition to their regular program.

How Can I Become a Provider?

Mental Health Providers, such as Psychiatrists, Psychologists, Social Workers, and Marriage and Family Therapists are trained to provide Psychotherapy. This enables them to guide a session so the client gets the most therapeutic benefit from the experience. To offer Animal Assisted Psychotherapy, the first criteria is to like and understand animals. The more familiar you are with animal behavior, the better your sessions will be. If you don't feel totally confident around animals, then it is best to work with an Animal Specialist you trust. It is really important to get to know, and be comfortable with, any animals you will be working with as your co-therapists.

It's very helpful to know each animal's different personality traits and be able to anticipate what behaviors to expect from them in various situations. This is important in planning your activities to ensure a successful outcome.

I have various animals with varying personalities and temperaments that bring out different issues with my clients. I have a cat that hides - which brings out isolation and loneliness issues in clients. I have a dog who likes to chew up paper - he's perfect for an activity where you want to "get rid of" negative issues. I have a pony that constantly wants to eat grass and won't walk without putting his head down to eat - how assertive do you need to be to move him? How does it feel to be ignored by him because he only wants the grass, or metaphorically speaking, the drugs if you're an addict? Is your pet shy, quiet, fearful? If so, how does your client feel about putting effort into the relationship to find the loving individual behind this façade? The answer may indicate how hard your client works at developing relationships with people. There is a similarity here!

The possibilities are endless. The activities can be guided by the personality of the pet you bring to the session.

There are training programs available for equine and pet assisted therapies through various organizations and schools. It may also be possible to work with an experienced provider and learn through on-the-job training. Understanding the animals you work with and understanding the human populations you work with are the basis and foundation for a good therapy program. The personality of the therapist is also a major factor. The session should always be thought provoking and positive. The clients should know that there are no right or wrong answers, that it's all about personal interpretations and growth. Animal Assisted Therapy is a personal experience to increase awareness of an individual's own strengths and weaknesses.

As a provider, there is one more business factor that needs to be addressed…insurance. You will most likely need liability and commercial insurance to protect yourself, your clients and your pets in the event of a mishap. There are not many insurance companies that offer this coverage, so it might be necessary to research it in your area to find what you need.

Personal Stories from Clients... The Impact of Pets

In one of my group activities, I asked participants to write about a personal pet experience...how it made them feel, how it changed them, and what effect it had on them long term. Here are some of the responses.

"My first time in equine therapy I tried to pick up the horse's foot. It wouldn't budge. I was confused because I thought horses lifted their feet easily and willingly. I was advised to pet and talk to the horse and then try again. Guess what? This time he lifted his leg! I learned that the relationship and trust have to come first."

"I went through a very tough week where I lost my job, broke up with my girlfriend and was miserable and depressed. My cat just wouldn't leave my side! It was really comforting and I didn't feel so alone."

"I never had a pet but my friend did. He had a really hyperactive, huge dog that I've known since he was a puppy and he never sits still. When I was going through a break up, he heard me crying and just lay there with me, letting me hold him until I was done. It was such a surprise and such a comfort."

"Taking care of my newborn puppy, having to make his formula and making sure he's not cold, taught me responsibility and helped me see why my parents care so much about my safety and health."

"When I get home, my dog lets me know he loves me because he barks until I say hi. Sometimes he comes over and asks me to play with him. It's such a nice feeling to be wanted."

"My dog always knew what time I got home from school and my mom said she'd always get up from wherever she was and move to be right by the garage door. So every day when I came home and opened the door to my house, she'd be sitting there with a huge smile for me!"

"My mom's cat would meow outside my door to come in my room. She would always wait for me to get home to go to bed and she slept with me every night. When she died, I was very upset. It really bothered me."

"I kicked the wife out and kept the dog. I enjoyed taking her fishing, to the park and on the boat. She was very comforting."

"During an equine therapy session, 2 horses near me got into a heated discussion and kicked out towards each other, which I found out is a warning sign among horses. The group pointed out that I didn't even move or react. I realized then that I was so used to being in an abusive family situation that I didn't even notice or try to protect myself from the potential danger. It was quite an eye opener for me!"

"I didn't know what to expect from Animal Assisted Psychotherapy when I went to my first group and I found it really fun to play with the 2 dogs there. We had a group discussion about the things you can learn from a dog and it gave me insight into some of my family relationships. I was pleasantly surprised to learn some new things about myself."

After the final session with a client in Equine Assisted Psychotherapy, I received this note, "Thank you for helping me enter into social settings. I find myself having an activity every day of the week. Once again, thank you for all your insight and direction. You have helped me to have the confidence to start living my life."

From the Pet's Perspective

Therapy involving animals adds an additional component that is not present in traditional therapy settings. It prompts an emotional response based on the human/animal interactions. Past experiences with animals, along with current experiences in the Animal Assisted Therapy setting, all become part of the therapy process. It's an opportunity for clients to look at their past relationships and explore new ones with the animals present in these sessions. Sometimes, we can get so focused on ourselves that we forget the animals have feelings and reactions too.

An interesting activity I have done involves asking people to write down how their pets would describe them and what their pets would say about them. While many hoped their pets would find them friendly, lovable and responsible, some have admitted that their pets also see them at their worst. They have shared stories of wonderful times together, as well as times they were unable to offer the care and attention their pets needed. In exploring this issue, they may be embarrassed or feel guilty and it helps them realize they need to make some life changes and improvements.

I have also asked what they think the animals are going through when they are engaging in Equine and Pet Assisted Therapy. This exercise helps increase people's awareness of others. It encourages them to think about someone else and pay attention to how others are feeling. They have to put themselves in someone else's shoes and see what that might be like. I have found that the different animals elicit different reactions and people's attitudes towards the animals change once they get to know and understand them better.

When people hold the snake, they are expecting him to try to get away, but they find that he seems quite content to curl up in a warm lap. They see that the rat is very sweet and engaging, and is happy to be picked up. She is curious about everything going on around her. The cats like the freedom to walk around and check people out. The dogs like to make the rounds visiting everybody. They seem to understand people's needs, and are content to sit by them for emotional support and give plenty of kisses. I have noticed that they spend more time with some people than with others, and have received feedback that they seem to sense who needs them the most. While the horses enjoy spending their time eating grass, they also like the attention of being brushed and interacting with people. When clients are involved in various activities with the horses they are often surprised at how responsive the horses are to them and their feelings.

All the animals genuinely enjoy interacting with people and look forward to "working".

My dogs know that when I put my bag of supplies by the door and put on their leashes, they are going to do Pet Assisted Therapy.

In the next photo, Bandit is barking at me to hurry up and Maggie is dancing around, ready to go. They are very excited and race to the car. When they arrive at the facility or the barn, they run out and greet everyone with their tails wagging.

Conclusion

My hope is that you now have a better understanding of what Animal Assisted Therapy is all about. It can help so many people in so many different aspects of personal and physical growth. Besides being so therapeutic, it's FUN! The animals enjoy it, the therapists enjoy it and the clients enjoy it! What could be better!

The Staff At Animals Bring Change

Carol Tannen, MSW, LCSW

David, Animal Specialist

Courtney, Animal Specialist

Kaya the Horse

Bandit the Dog

Bentley the Dog

Maggie the Dog

Chloe the Cat

Duke the Cat

Rahj the Cat

Arcturus the Snake

Ratilda the Rat

Staff Photos

Carol, Kaya and David enjoying lunch together

Rahj and Bandit hanging out

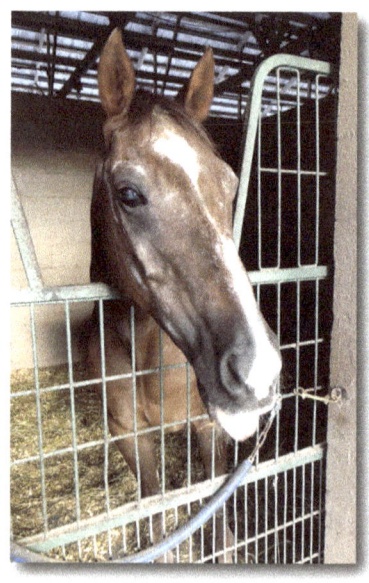

Kaya talking to us

Kaya happily grazing

 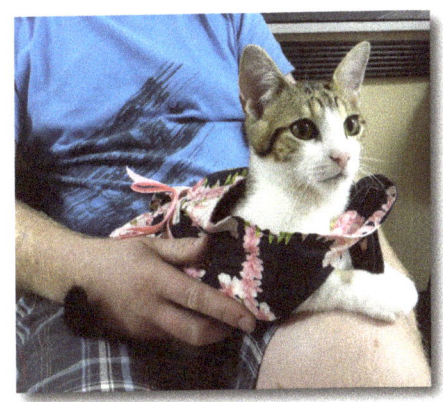

Duke and Rahj putting up with these outfits

Bandit and Ratilda
sharing leftovers

Maggie and Ratilda
hanging out

Maggie—I love my fancy coat!

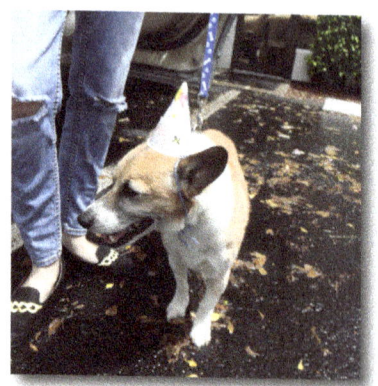
Bandit-Happy Birthday to me!

Bandit celebrating a Happy 4th of July!

Chloe and Bandit Chilling

Arcturus on the move

Ratilda kissing Maggie on the cheek

Kaya loving life!

Courtney on Kaya

David and Kaya enjoying a sunset ride at the barn

Staff relaxing
after a hard day at work

About the Author

Carol Tannen has been a Clinical Social Worker for over 40 years, has had pets all of her life, and has been riding horses since she was a young girl. She received her Master's Degree in Social Work in 1975 from Syracuse University. She has worked in a variety of settings, including a psychiatric in-patient hospital, a residential geriatric facility, an outpatient counseling center, a halfway house for mentally challenged teens, and most recently, in farm and office locations incorporating various animals into the therapy sessions. She has worked with many different populations including the elderly, families, children, individuals, groups, people struggling with addiction and eating disorders, and those with physical and mental disabilities.

Throughout her lifetime, Carol has enjoyed the companionship of numerous loving animals....cats, dogs, horses, chickens, ducks, guinea pigs, turtles, hamsters, birds, rabbits, fish, a snake and a rat. Caring for and interacting with so many different kinds of pets led her to become a Veterinary Assistant in 2002.

In 1993 she was very excited to own her first horse, a 6 year old quarter horse named Main Kaya. At 32 he is still going strong. Kaya's vet attributes his longevity to "good genes", but Carol would like to think that her taking good care of him over the past 26 years has also been a factor and has had something to do with it! Partnering with Kaya, she has attended many workshops in Natural Horsemanship. She has also worked with several therapists certified in Equine Assisted Therapy. Her dual training in Natural Horsemanship and Equine Assisted Therapy enables her to be very comfortable working alongside the horses while focusing on the needs of the participants in the program.

Carol has blended her Social Work skills with her love of animals to provide Equine and Animal Assisted Therapy to those in need of positive change since 2010. Her therapy benefits individuals, couples, families, groups, people with eating disorders, people with drug and alcohol dependency, children with various disabilities, and corporations wishing to strengthen staff relationships.

Carol's latest venture has been designing animal themed rings. She calls them "Honor Rings" to Honor the cherished relationship between people and their animals. The cat, dog and horse rings are made of sterling silver and have bright golden stones in the eyes and tails to represent the sunshine that animals bring into our lives.

They all come in a gift box with the following poem attached as a gift card:

To Honor Cherished Moments

With: (pet's name goes here)
When I wear this HONOR RING
With these stones shining bright,
I think of you with joy and delight.
The sparkle and Sunshine
You've brought into my heart
Brightens my thoughts
Whether we're together or apart.
This ring is a reminder
Of all that we share,
And to HONOR our relationship
And show how much I care.
From: (your name goes here)

It's quite obvious that Carol cares deeply about both people and animals.

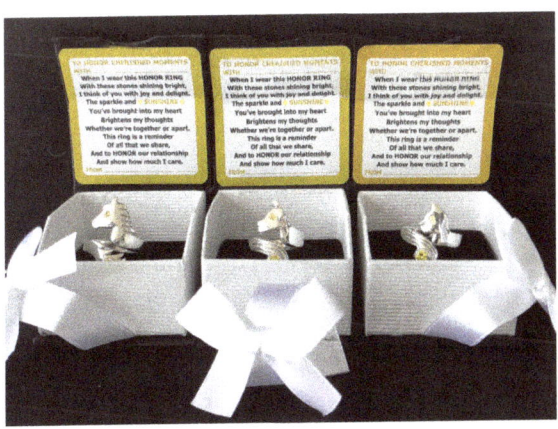

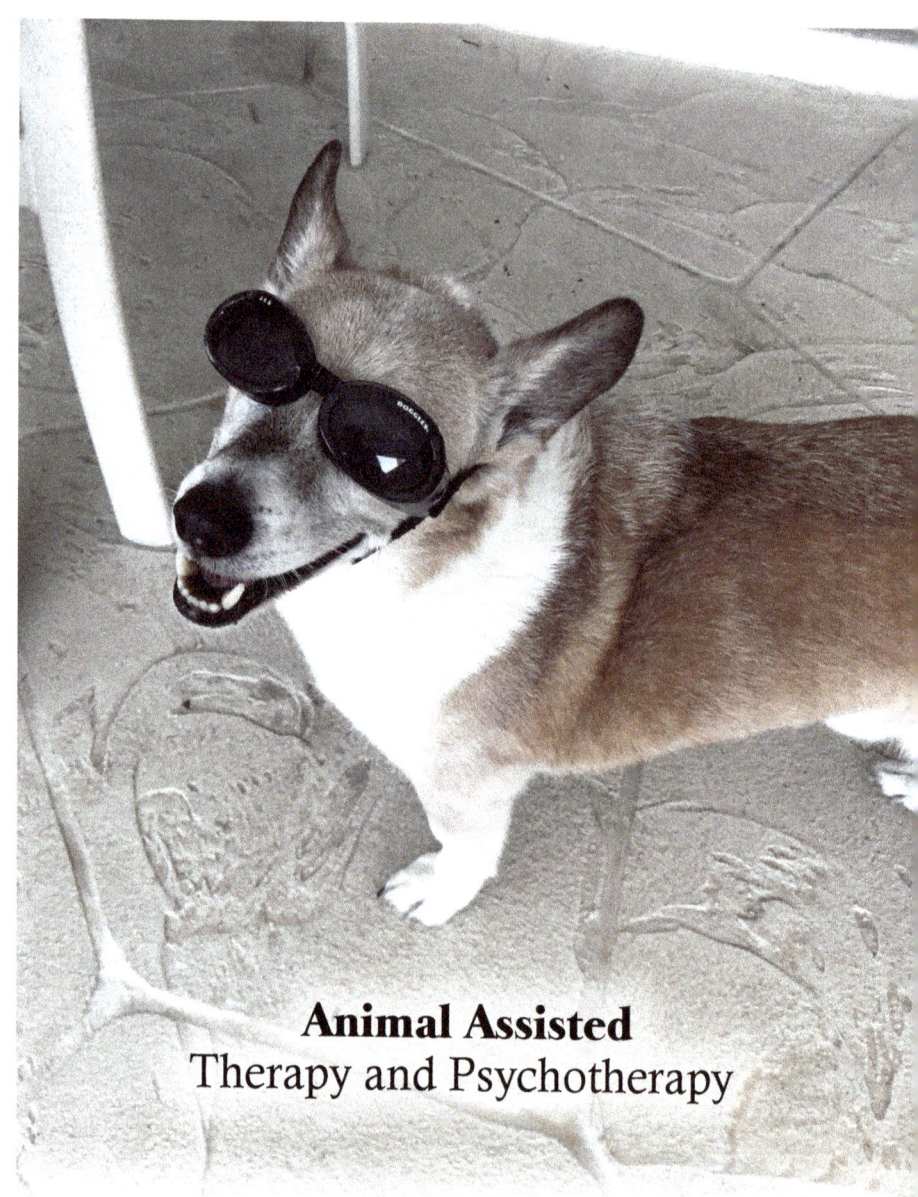

Animal Assisted Therapy and Psychotherapy

ANIMALS BRING CHANGE

The ABC's of personal growth through Equine and Pet Assisted Psychotherapy

ctzoo@aol.com
www.AnimalsBringChange.com

www.ingramcontent.com/pod-product-compliance
Lightning Source LLC
Chambersburg PA
CBHW051552010526
44118CB00022B/2677